# Letting You Go

Tianna Page

ISBN: 9798682561735

# DEDICATION

Dedicated to the people who feel too much and too little, all at the same time.

# ACKNOWLEDGMENTS

First, I want to thank all of the wonderful people in my life who encouraged me to create something magical and who cheered the loudest when I told them I wanted to publish. I would especially like to thank Bronte Waite and Laura McNab-Coombs for reading unfinished poems, for providing feedback, for letting me bounce ideas off of them, and for being an endless source of support and love. I would like to thank my parents, Len and Teresa Delorie, for encouraging me to read and write as a child, and for hounding me endlessly to write poetry (even when I didn't think I was a poet). Finally, I would like to thank my amazing partner, Tyler Cooper, for the three amazing words he said when I told him I wanted to publish a poetry book: it's about time.

# Letting You Go

There is freedom in letting go

of something that once brought tears of joy to your eyes

and effortless smiles to your lips,

because now it brings breathless sobs

and anxiety.

There is peace in accepting the heartache and hurt.

You are opening yourself

to something more beautiful

## Stifled & Starved

two years ended

in two minutes

because no matter how I bent

or forced

or contorted

I could not shape myself to fit you

but, God, how I tried

for so long

to carve out the pieces and parts

you didn't love

to cut off old stems

to make room for new growth

but instead I stopped growing

stifled and starved

for sunlight

# Dolly's & Daddies

I was told

not to get a back tattoo

because how would I receive

the needle they shove into you

if a tattoo marred my body

I was told

I must play with dolls

to practice for a life

I did not sign up for

that I did not agree to

I was told

to find a man

and settle down

to take his last name

and give him babies

I was told

I was told

I was told

but you do not make my choices for me

# Resiliency

I took the plunge

jumped off the deepest ledge

and plummeted to the ground

I hoped I would gain wings

in the fall

I hoped I would be saved

but now my bones shatter

and break

as I lay

cast aside

but I haven't stopped growing

my flesh melts into the earth

my blood waters the dirt

daisies grow out of my chest

and eyes

it is amazing how resilient we are

# Believing

You ask if I believe in soul mates

I never have,

but I'm starting to

# You Don't Get to Keep Me

you don't get to keep

the parts of me

that make you feel better

that make you feel alive

while you discard the parts

that don't suit you

the parts that are challenging

and hard to love

the parts you decided aren't worth it anymore


you don't get to keep me

I have stopped loving

every man that came before you

you won't be any different


-   **Time Apart**

## Sleep in Peace

look for me

deep in the forest

where the trees

grow so tightly

no sunlight peeks through

and in the darkness

we can sleep

in peace

# Feel Something

I thought I met an equal who could discuss poetry and art, the intricacies of life after death, the unfathomable empires of our minds (I want you to feel something). I thought I met a kindred spirit, because everything flowed so freely between us, like our souls were very old friends who jumped at the chance to reunite (why won't you feel something?). Yet now, when I speak, or sing, or write, you are motionless and quiet, with cheap platitudes and thoughts, and I get so angry when you refuse, because I thought you matched my intensity, I thought you matched my passion, I thought art moved you the way it moves me, and at the very least I thought I moved you (I need you to fucking feel something).

this compulsory longing

these incessant

and intrusive thoughts

about your lips,

hands

caressing mine,

this obsessive need

to love

and be loved

by you

**- limerence**

## **Are You Happy Now?**

I hope you're happy

with a life

of unending cycles

where every single day

is the exact same

and nothing you do

changes anything

I hope you're happy

with monotony

and boredom

and loneliness

I hope it eats into your heart

and festers

leaving holes

in the places

I used to be

I hope you're happy

I think of her

and I am lost

all thoughts scatter

and I forget how to breathe

trying to categorize

the colour of her heart


**- Passionfruit**

## Seeing God

your lips touched mine

and you coaxed

the moans

from my tongue,

brushed fingers

down my spine,

and whispered

that you felt

closest to God

when you moved in me,

introduced me to heaven,

and showed me

what it's like

to have a religious experience

# Melancholy

Some days I just want to sleep

I want to take pill after pill

and spend the day in bed

no dreams

no thoughts

no noise

like a tiny taste of death

without the finality


some days are unbearable

and no matter how hard I try

to force myself to get up

and do the things that make me better

it is so much easier to give in

to try again tomorrow

with fresh eyes

a fresh start

I need a break from myself

# A Certain Type of Man

you sit at home

confused,

hurt,

and guilty,

because you want to be the type of man

that sits next to her

and thinks only of her,

but instead

you think of me,

and you hate yourself,

you hate yourself,

and maybe even hate me, too.

## Ugly Words

I sit on the bathroom floor

back pressed up against the cold hard bathtub

sobs breaking from my chest

eyes swollen and stinging.


You don't want me.


If there are four uglier words I do not know them.

# The Rose Wallpaper

There is a rip at the bottom of the rose wallpaper

not enough to see behind

just small enough to notice

the tiny film of pink and gold

raising along the edges

I ignore it for a time

try to avoid it

the best I can

but day by day

the paper spreads

into tiny spider veins

and the wallpaper pulls

up

up

up

until I can't take it anymore

so I grab a pair of pliers and begin to peel that paper back, ripping tiny little pieces, tiny little chunks, over and over again, until the walls are torn apart and rose coloured heaps litter the floor.

now the walls are grey

and mute

all colour has disappeared

it is bleak

and empty

how utterly disappointing

## Value

I used to think

what I said

didn't have value,

that it fell

on deaf ears

because of how

unimportant

I am,

and no matter

how I spoke

or screamed,

nothing changed

and no one heard

but that was a cage

I created for myself

and allowed others

to lock me in

now I know

the voice I have,

and the words I speak,

have value

and meaning,

not because others decided,

but because I did

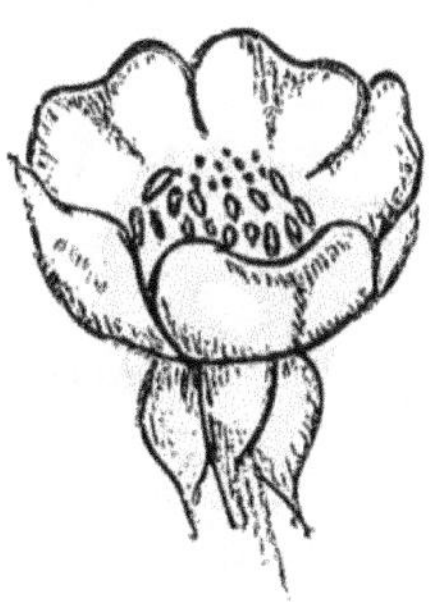

# Into the Forest

lay me down with the moss

by an old willow tree

where wildflowers grow

through the cracks in my skin

where sunlight warms my cold hands

and butterflies live in my skull

lay me down in the forest

by an old cedar tree

where mushrooms grow over

my lungs and my feet

where moonlight glows on my collarbones

and bats make a home from my chest

lay me down in the grass

by an old oak tree

where graves are unmarked

and we're just left to be

# The Unrelenting Lock

There is a small, beautiful chest

with ornate patterns

and carvings

and a tiny brass lock.

Inside are treasures and trinkets,

everything you've ever wanted,

everything you've ever dreamed of,

but the key is long gone:

given away,

haphazardly,

so many years before.


You refuse to smash the chest,

or set it on fire,

or cut off the lock.

No.

You're too clever for that.

You know a different way.

A different approach.

You will coax and touch the lock

until it gives away its secrets,

because you know

precisely

the whispered words

to say


you work all of your magic,

pour everything you have

to seize the treasure within


yet the lock is unrelenting

it holds steady and fast.


but you will not be beaten,

each day you do the same:

whisper

coax

touch

finally, sweet finally,

the lock can hear your whispers

it knows you deeply now

intimate

loving

it is ready

to open

and let you inside


this is the moment you've worked for. Waited for. The moment
things change. The greatest show. The big bang. The celebratory
screams. The peanut-crunching crowd gather round to hear:

but oh,

what a shame

what a shame


the chest is empty

## Saving Each Other

I catch reflections of myself in his wounded blue eyes

the way we feel pain

deeply and all encompassing

is the same.

I have never met a man who understands melancholy

the way I do.

I am intoxicated by his broken

addicted to his pain

because when he touches me

it doesn't hurt so much

## Needy

I want you to wrap me in your arms

and hold me

when I can't outrun the monsters

that feast inside my head

I want you to kiss my lips

when they tremble

from the acid that I spew

I want you to drown out all my thoughts

before I drown myself

and I want you to love me when I'm breaking

and don't know how to love

# Starlight

your lips

taste like starlight

and sadness,

such an intoxicating mix

of beauty and pain

## Greedy

you told me

there wasn't room for me

that you barely had time

and could give me nothing


and I just nodded

because I was desperate to be near you

desperate to know you

even if it meant

countless nights

wondering why I'm not enough


I thought a tiny piece of you

was better than nothing

if only I knew

how greedy I would become

# Careless

I leave my glass heart at the doorstep, because what we do behind closed doors,

barred windows, with empty eyes, is

careless.

I strip down at the doorstep, leave my fragile soul behind, and give myself to you:

an empty vessel, dead inside,

lifeless eyes.

But you don't mind my cold hands, my still chest.

You are lonely.

And so we lie, side by side, hollow and broken together.

## Something Pretty

I wanted to write you something pretty

about twin fires,

colliding stars,

but I scratch and scribble out

every line


I wanted to tell you how I feel

about soul mates,

predestined fate,

but words fail me

whenever you're around


know that I love you

and will never be the same

## Aligning Stars

I have taken our stars from the heavens

and placed them in a glass jar.

Now I can examine

the fault,

the curse,

the flaw.

I can relive every moment

of silence,

agony,

and hurt.


but, wait.


Our stars are not faulty,

not cursed,

not flawed.

I have searched them,

devoured them:

thorough,

desperate.


The truth is much sadder,

much worse:


the stars are not ours.

## Trust Issues

over and over

I tell myself to trust you

I tell myself to believe that someone like you

could love someone

as fucked up as me.


but the voice inside my head

is so much louder

than the times you whisper

I love you

and the self-hatred

and self-doubt

drown out

the times

you promised I mean something.


I'm not used to being special.

I don't know how to love.

# Laughter

the first time you kissed me

I laughed,

not because there was anything

inherently funny

about the way you held me,

but because I imagined that moment

so many times

I couldn't comprehend

the reality of your lips on mine,

and I couldn't help

the little bubble of laughter

that escaped,

because I wanted you to spend the rest of the night,

the rest of all nights,

tasting my laughter.

I do not mind

that I am hard to love

a challenge

a work in progress

because it simply

weeds out

those that cannot meet me on my level

those that I am all too happy to leave.


give me a lover

born from chaos and gloom

who will stand beside me

and rise from the dust


**- chaos and gloom**

# Beautiful Day

one day you'll run into him

at your favourite café or theatre

and you'll be amazed

by how little you feel;

you won't remember the sound of his laugh,

you won't remember the taste of his demons,

just two strangers passing by

with a polite nod

or smile.

you'll no longer write poems about his hands,

because you don't know how they touch anymore,

and it will be a beautiful, beautiful day.

## Good Enough

My flaws sit at the tip of my tongue

ready to spill from my mouth

at any second

but I bite down on that poison

and force myself to swallow.


I am good enough.


repeat that until your voice is hoarse.


I am good enough.

## Hold Me

And when I cannot leave our bed

do not ask why

or say you understand

       just hold me

# Your Name

The stars keep me up,

because they whisper your name,

and since I don't have the strength

to say it anymore

I lie awake and listen,

hoping the stars still haunt you, too

## Fuck-ups and Flaws

It is easier to strike, lash out,

and hurt you so badly you never want to return,

because the thought of you leaving on your own,

deciding you no longer want

my fuck-ups and flaws

is unbearable.

It is selfish, I know,

to love the brokenness in him,

to want to heal him because I cannot heal myself.

He is selfish, too,

to love the colour of my heart,

because his own is grey and dulling.

This is just another trait we have in common:

all we share are flaws.


**- Selfish**

It doesn't happen all at once.

It happens over time.

Memory by memory.

Inch by inch.

I give it all back to you:

the conversations of life and death,

the vulnerable moments of anxiety and panic,

the first time you tasted my laughter.

You can have it all back.

I release them to you.

This is how I let you go.

**- how to let go**

## Indecisive

We often ask and wonder:

if your house was on fire,

what would you grab?

For many it is simple:

their pets

their pictures

their passports,

but I just laugh and nod,

because I know myself too well.

I would stand between rooms,

running back and forth,

too indecisive to save anything,

and dying in the process.

## Prison

deep inside my heart

there is a box

where I have locked up

all thoughts

and memories of you

and though I say you'll always have space

you should know that it's not pleasant

## Forgetting You

Forgetting you is painful

the type of pain you feel deep in your stomach

like being punched so hard

you're winded

and nauseous

and light headed

all at the same time.


Remembering you feels the same.

# Empty

I cannot forget the sound of your laugh,

not because it's burned inside my mind,

forever etched into my soul,

but because you never laughed freely,

and you never smiled easily.

You are controlled.

Tame.

Unable to express or feel joy.

And in a lover that is something

I cannot bear.


I thought I could help you.

I thought I could make you happy.

But I cannot make an empty man feel anything.

# Hell

I have committed the worst crime,

my father,

allowed the poison you spat

to sink into my veins


fire and ash

fire and ash


I have plotted against you,

my father,

made stories of your horror,

picked the scars you left behind


fire and ash

fire and ash


but I am not broken like you,

my father,

I can speak without screaming,

touch without bruising,

love without destroying.


fire and ash

fire and ash


If there is a hell, my father,

you are in it.

# Force of Nature

I do not need another person to complete me.

There is a hurricane inside my soul

fire in my stomach

tsunamis in my eyes


I am all that I need

an irrevocable force of nature

## Destruction & Rebirth

The longer I go without touching you

the better his touch will feel.

It will not feel cold,

lifeless,

shallow,

my dry lips begging his tongue to ignite something within me.

He does not bring me to life like you.

He does not destroy me like you either.

# Find Your Way Back

find me in the trees

wandering through the shadows

and leaves

I'll carry a lantern, my love,

so you can find you way back to me


find me in the trees

walking hand-in-hand

with the butterflies and bees

I'll save you a dance, my love,

when you make your way back to me


find me in the trees

laying down in the grass

where time starts to creep

I've waited so long, my love,

have you lost your way back to me?

## Cowardice & Compliments

the lips that kiss your scars

part to call you a coward


the hands that cradle your face

slap and scratch and push


I am the cancer

and the cure

keeping you together

and tearing you apart

## Choices

You no longer call me happiness

or sweetheart

talk about my passionfruit heart

or the way I light up

every aspect of your hollow life


but you can fuck me

and get your fill

until I have nothing left to give

and then you try to say

I chose this

## **Breaking My Own Heart**

I have done the unthinkable

grabbed my heart back from you

pressed it in my hands

and squeezed until it shattered

the splinters and shards cut deep

slicing into the fingers that should have held onto you

blood runs down my body and arms

soaking into the knees that should have begged you to fight

pools form at the feet that want so desperately to run back to you.


Why did I think it would be easier to break my own heart?

I should have let you do it

# Reminiscing

We ran barefoot through the trees

and alleys,

jumped from ledges

into puddles,

rode our bikes

down steep hills,

chased boys

then ran faster,

we danced under stars

whispered dreams to the moon

we escaped all of our demons,

we ran barefoot through the trees

## Insecurity

deep down

we are both incapable of love:

too selfish,

too scared,

too screwed up.

So we cling to one another,

suffocating,

with hollow words

spilling from our lips:

promises we don't mean,

don't intend to keep.

I am crazy about you.


Or maybe,

just crazy.

you bring the sun with you

wherever you go

you create light in the darkness

and banish all shadow

it is warm in your presence

because you drive the cold away

it is magic

how you chase away the emptiness

**-you bring the sun with you**

# Grand Finale

This is how we fall apart:

not in one final scene

the grand finale

the tragic ending

but in tiny little moments

of hatred and hurt

# Religion

I have known your demons:

how they make your chest burn,

your lungs collapse;

how badly you wish you could die.


I have held your demons,

let them bite, claw, and defile me,

sacrificed myself over and over

to save an ounce of your skin.


I have fought your demons,

but I couldn't let them die,

because you felt more real,

as fucked up as myself.


I have loved your demons,

worshiped at their altar,

gained salvation in their touch,

it feels like sacrilege.

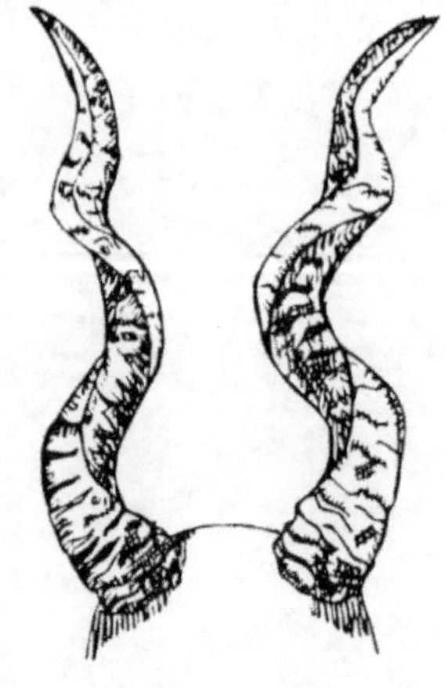

## Delicate Flower

I take a deep breath.

I have missed you,

this part of myself

I've hidden away for so long.


I am not a delicate flower.

I am the storm that destroys them,

rips their petals off,

and leaves them crumpled on the ground,

dying.

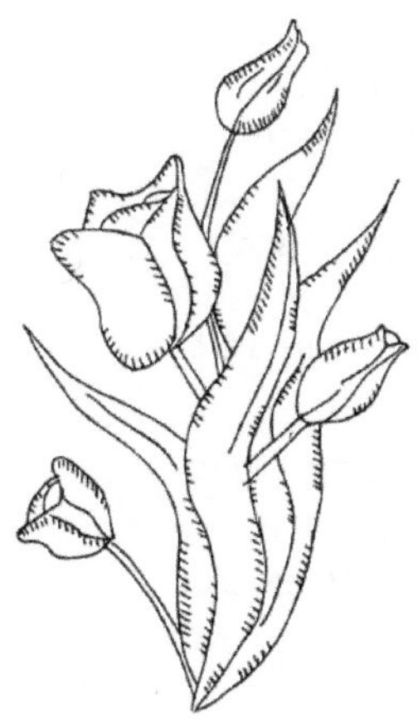

# Flames & Dust

i struck a match

and burned

every laugh and kiss

your poisonous touch

until flames surrounded me

i peeled off my skin

let it bubble

and boil

desperate

to possess a body

you have not invaded

but i am not a Phoenix.

there is no resurrection

born again from ash and soot

because fire cannot clean

the marks you left on me


i am nothing but dust now

## Absence

I am looking for someone to erase you

I want his touch to burn away all the fingerprints you left behind

I want something

anything

to replace the heaviness of your absence

# Timing

in one instant it clicked into place:

the distance

the silence

the repetition of my constant questions

is it time yet?

is it time yet?

is our time yet?

but the excuses came easy

wrapped in sickly-sweet words

and promises

our time will never come

in one instant it clicked into place.

we are so scared

to be the one

that loves more,

the one

that gets hurt,

but isn't it beautiful

knowing the depth you can love to?

knowing the horrors you can survive?

And isn't it heartbreaking

that some people will never comprehend

all the love you can give?


**- Courage**

## Take me with you

we talk about grand adventures

exploring and leaving

going anywhere

running as far and as fast as we can


yet it is from this life we want to run

from the monotony of everyday experiences

and people

from the isolation and burden

of our own minds

and deep down

I know that when you run

I cannot follow

# Human

I have never felt as safe and warm

as I did with you,

and I didn't know the intensity that I could love

or be loved with

until you held me, wrapped me up,

breathed light into spaces I kept dark for so long,

and brought me back to life with every stitch and seam.


you made me feel human,


you made me feel worthy.

# Ricochet

I lay in bed

and pick apart my flaws:


how effortlessly

I teeter back and forth

between extremes.


I am too affectionate,

yet incapable of love:

my lips part to remind you

that I adore every detail of your face

that beautiful, cold face,

yet later, while I fuck other men,

I do not think of you.


I cannot get enough of you,

or I cannot wait for you to leave.

I want to crush your hand in mine,

feel your heartbeat through my skin,

beg you to never let go,

while I scratch and claw and push,

and tell you you're unworthy.


I ricochet

I ricochet

I ricochet

## Wish You Well

you came into my life

just when I needed you

     and while some people are meant to stay

     others are not

there is no more anger or sadness

just two souls who have learned as much

as they can from each other

and because I know this is not our time

I'll send you love and light

and wish you well on your way


because now is the time to learn

from someone new

we must grow and change in different directions

yet always towards the sun

it's okay to let me go now

with fondness

without regret

think of me when the sun shines through the trees

send me light and love

and wish me well on my way

think of me when the sun shines through the trees

send me light and love

and wish me well on my way

# Your poem

one day you'll read this poem

and all the others

and you'll wonder

which ones are about you

and you'll wonder how you managed

to destroy

yet motivate me


So, this is your poem.


each line and letter were written just for you.

how does it feel

knowing you've inspired greatness

from a heart you won't ever touch again?

## "Please Don't Leave for Good"

the moment I heard those words

I knew they would haunt

my thoughts and my heart

that I would write poem

after poem

about the vulnerability

and sadness

you hide behind

and I know this destroys

us both

yet I cannot stay

    forgive me

for thinking our hearts

fit together

    forgive me

for leaving this way

# Tethered

tell me we've run out

of second chances

that there is no hope

for a future

or a life together

      tell me you don't want me anymore

because I need you to let me go

and I can't go far if I'm tethered

      freedom is a gift

      let me go

## Father's Daughter

I do not want you to look at me

and see his eyes

but if you knew what I have done

you would call me my father's daughter

cry about apples and trees

and wonder

how you raised someone

so beautiful

yet toxic

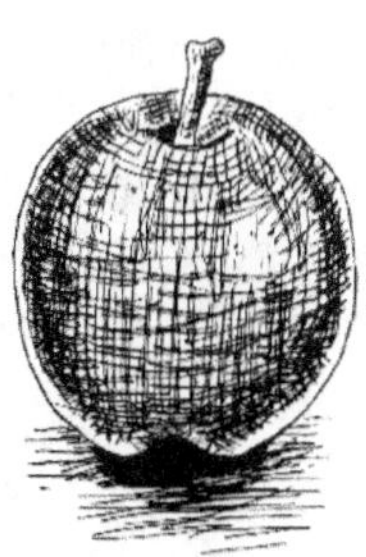

# Harm

judgmental

mean-spirited

you hurl these words

as if they have any leverage

as if they have any power over me


I've heard it all before

and much worse

I've said it all before

and much worse


call me every name you can think of,

because you could never do more harm

than I've already done to myself

## Good and Bad Days

You don't talk to him anymore. Sometimes you even forget about him, for a moment, at least, while your mind is distracted by other things. You go a full day without crying. Then you go two. You catch yourself smiling at strangers on the street, lovers holding hands; you get great news and you don't even think about calling him.

and then there are the days when it hits you

and you crumple and break

wondering why you can't stop loving him

why no one catches your attention like him

why his touch sets every inch of you on fire

leaving you numb to anyone else

you pull over to the side of the road

just so you can sob and sob and sob

without thinking of steering yourself

into oncoming traffic

# Safe with Me

keep my heart safe

even as you let me go,

because you leave with a piece of me

and a piece of you stays with me, too


that's the beauty of love:

we never seem to run out of pieces to give

no matter how many times we break or crumple

we are an infinite source of magic


so, you may keep that part of my heart

and I'll keep yours, too

it will be safe with me

even as I let you go

## Creating Space

I convince myself I know what's best

I give space

I create distance

ignore texts and calls

for hours and hours

give the appearance that I'm busy

far too busy

but I'm drowning in silence

I convince myself I know what's best

# Comparing You to Him

you showed me I could love

with an intensity I thought died

the moment he did


so I compared you to him,

built you up in my head,

because for one brief second it felt like he had returned,

like I had a second chance to save him,

if I could only save you, too


but he was never cruel the way you are.

he never cut me apart with silence and worry.

he never made me feel unlovable.


the comparisons have to end,

not because they are fictitious or wrong,

but because you are not worthy of his title

you are not worthy of that piece of my heart that belonged to him.


however, I am thankful you reminded me:

I can love with an intensity I thought died

the moment he did

## Cancerous

I am invading his body,

making it hard to think of anything else,

changing his life,

kept like a secret carcinoma,

every poison-laden kiss:

He calls me toxic.

# I Remember How You Made Me Feel

I can barely remember your laugh

I barely recall if your eyes were golden like a sunset

or brown like the roots and the trees

and as each year passes

I get older

and older

but you stay the same

immortalized in pictures and poems


you will never have crow's feet

or laugh lines

you will never watch me walk down the aisle, dressed in white

and each year I lose more of you

each year your voice fades


but I remember how you made me feel

I remember dancing in the kitchen

wrapped in your arms

homemade birthday cards

and hand-written poems

and even though your presence fades

these feelings never will

## Silent Phone Calls

we stayed on the phone

for as long as we could,

because we both knew the minute it ended,

we did, too,

and we feared what came after,

too scared to say goodbye,

so, we sat in silence,

letting the minutes pass by,

grieving the end

of an era.

# Medicine/What if

when I cry

or talk about

the chaos in my mind

he tells me

to call my doctor

to get medicine

to help

because I cannot help myself


and yet I argue.

I blame the weather.

I blame the cold.

I blame my fucked-up predispositions.


because I am terrified

to lose my edge

to lose my muse

the way I feel happiness now

is all consuming and euphoric


what if this isn't normal?

what if the medicine changes who I am?


or what if it's even worse


what if I don't change at all?

## Pretty

I look around the cold room.

My mouth is ready to open, ready to say my first words.


but you, my creator, shake your head.

Shhh.

silly thing.

you are so pretty,

with your blonde hair,

blue eyes,

full lips.

why, everyone knows dolls can't speak.


but I don't want to be pretty.

I want to be wild.

Intelligent.

Kind.


you pick up a needle and laugh while you speak:

you were made to be pretty,

all the other dolls will hate you,

that's how pretty you are.


But what good will it do If they hate me?

How will I make any friends?


you sigh.

not this again.

why aren't you dolls ever happy?

don't you see all I have done for you?

why must you always need more?

It should be enough that you're pretty.

You forced me to do this.


you grab my arms

and pin them to my sides;

the needle pierces my skin,

rips through my cheeks,

as your fingers move through me.

my lips are sewn shut,

stained red by my blood.

but isn't

red pretty?

# Weak-hearted Men Beware:

I will set your soul on fire,

burn so bright and hot,

that when I leave

the cold will seep into the crevasses and cracks

that I created,

and you will wonder how you ever survived the flames

## Sharp Edges

When I'm with him

I am normal,

less fucked up,

like all of my edges are softer

and they no longer cut the fingers

that try to piece them back together


but when I'm with you,

Oh, God,

when I'm with you,

it's okay that blood stains your fingertips,

because my hands look the same,

and we cut ourselves

over

and

over

again,

running our fingers along sharp edges

## One Thousand Times

I have searched

one thousand different lives

to find you

and I have called you

one thousand different names

known one thousand different eyes

touched one thousand different hands

but nothing changes

I have loved one heart

one soul

one thousand times

I am whole

and I have value

even if you don't see it


**- with or without you**

## Armor

I apologize

over and over again

because lately every time I open my mouth

poison spills out

and eats away at the armor

I built you

and I don't know how to stop

the venom that I spit

I don't know how to stop

my mean spirit


the ground is too far from this pedestal

I think the fall might kill me

## Us

I don't believe in soul mates

or destiny,

but I believe in us.

I believe in two people making it work,

two people choosing,

day after day,

that what we have is precious,

and so unbearably worth it,

that even our worst days

are still better

than the days we spend apart.

you love me more

now that it's over

and the irony

tastes delicious

- **I love you less**

# Duet

she takes up space in my mind

like a parasite

or a tick

and no matter what I do

she's always there

(I cannot escape her, because she's a runner, too, and she's faster)


I question what you say,

I wonder how many times she's heard the same,

because honey drips so smoothly from your lips

you must have practice

(I hear her voice when I sing, she plays along on the piano)


I search for her in pictures

and voicemails,

like a mad scientist

I have brought this woman to life,

created from small snippets,

this mesmerizing creature

haunts my thoughts,

my writing,

my heart

I wonder if I haunt her, too.

does she flinch when you say my name?

does she wonder what makes me so special?

because I see her reflection in your eyes

and I bet she sees mine, too.

# The Cycle

we were created to love

and break

and heal

and do it all again.

each time feels worse than the last,

and we swear,

swear to any god that will listen,

that we won't put ourselves through it,

that we won't ever give ourselves again,

but we do.

we always do.

our resiliency is stunning,

the way we stitch ourselves together,

take our broken shards and pieces

and forge them into something new,

because deep down we know:

we were created to love

and break

and heal

and do it all again.

# ABOUT THE AUTHOR

Tianna Page is a Canadian poet living in British Columbia. She has a Bachelor's degree in Psychology and English and a Diploma in Creative Writing. She's been writing since a young age and has always dreamt of publishing. Some of her favourite poets include: Pablo Neruda, Anne Sexton, Sylvia Plath and Rupi Kaur. Her seventh – and possibly favourite – tattoo is a line from Sylvia Plath's 'Lady Lazarus' across her collarbone. When Tianna isn't writing she enjoys travelling, painting, drawing, and spending time with her loved ones (particularly her two dogs).

If you want to stay up to date with Tianna's work you can find her on Instagram: @tiannapagepoetry